TO THE TEACHER

T0081467

In my many years of teaching piano to the young I have found that the theory of music, so necessary for good performance and musicianship, is best learned and **retained** through written work.

The lessons herewith have been used with excellent results and at the request of countless teachers met during my many workshops I am now making them available herewith in printed form.

They are designed to supply written work that will make plainer than plain the facts in learning about music. Actually, theory is the language of music and to perform well one must speak and understand this "language" without hestitation.

The written work will not only train the student to observe carefully and to be accurate in what he does but will also serve as a help to the teacher in checking the student's comprehension of what he is learning.

The work progresses gradually and is planned to be suitable for use with any method or series of teaching materials either in class or private instruction.

It is suggested that these lessons be given the student one at a time.

EDNA MAE BURNAM

ISBN 978-1-4234-0531-3

EXCLUSIVELY DISTRIBUTED BY

HAL•LEONARD®

Visit Hal Leonard Online at
www.halleonard.com

Contact us:
Hal Leonard
7777 West Bluemound Road
Milwaukee, WI 53213
Email: info@halleonard.com

In Europe, contact:
Hal Leonard Europe Limited
42 Wigmore Street
Marylebone, London, W1U 2RN
Email: info@halleonardeurope.com

In Australia, contact:
Hal Leonard Australia Pty. Ltd.
4 Lentara Court
Cheltenham, Victoria, 3192 Australia
Email: info@halleonard.com.au

The music writing work in BOOK THREE is built on the following musical facts:

NOTES

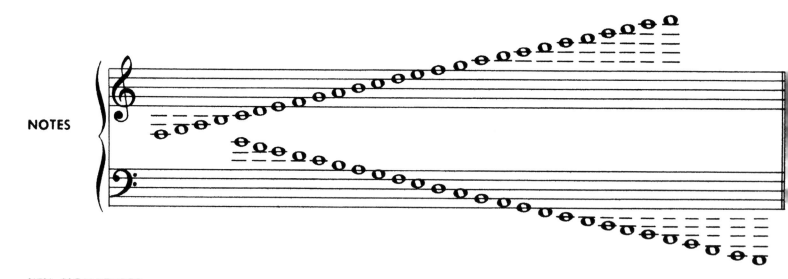

KEY SIGNATURES

C MAJOR	G MAJOR	D MAJOR	A MAJOR	E MAJOR
F MAJOR	Bb MAJOR	Eb MAJOR	Ab MAJOR	

TIME SIGNATURES

NOTE AND REST VALUES

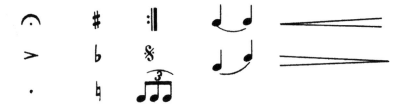

MUSICAL SIGNS

MUSICAL WORDS AND ABBREVIATIONS

DOLCE	ANDANTE
MARCATO	ALLEGRO
GIOCOSO	MODERATO
TEMPO	RIT.
LEGATO	DIM.
STACCATO	CRESC.
FINE	ACCEL.

STEPS AND PATTERNS

HALF STEPS
WHOLE STEPS
MAJOR SCALES AND PATTERNS

BOOK THREE
LESSON ONE

Pupil's Name _____ Date _____ Grade (or Star) _____

1. READING

READ THIS HELPER ALOUD!

Notes not printed on the staff are printed on LEGER lines and spaces in the same order as notes printed on the staff.

Study these leger lines and spaces.

C B A G F

C D E F G

As you read these notes, print their letter names in the boxes above and below them.

2. WRITING

HELPER. Three new musical words.

Dolce . . . . softly and sweetly
Giocoso . . . . gay and happy
Marcato . . . . march time and style

Write the musical words for the following meanings:

gay and happy _____

march time and style _____

softly and sweetly _____

3. SPELLING

Spell these words.
Print them in the boxes under the notes.

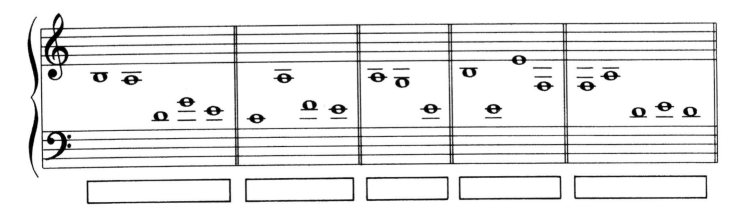

HELPER

♪ (one sixteenth note) = ¼ beat.

♪ (one sixteenth rest) = ¼ beat.

♬♬ (four sixteenth notes) = 1 beat.

(four sixteenth rests) = 1 beat.

♬ (two sixteenth notes) = ½ beat.

♬♬ (four sixteenth notes) = 1 quarter note.

♬ (two sixteenth notes) = 1 eighth note.

4. COUNTING

Put in the bar lines and number the counting in each measure.

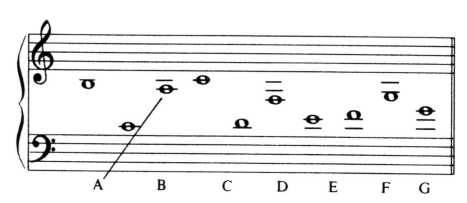

5. DRAWING

Draw a line from each note to the correct letter name.

A   B   C   D   E   F   G

6. GAME

CROSSWORD PUZZLE

Print the correct word in the PUZZLE that the CUE LIST calls for.

PUZZLE

CUE LIST

Down ↓

1. The end.
2. Softly and sweetly.
3. March time and style.

Across →

4. Gay and happy.
5. Time.
6. Slowly.

LESSON TWO

Pupil's Name _____ Date _____ Grade (or Star) _____

1. *READING*

READ THIS ALOUD!

This is the Key Signature of A MAJOR.

There are three sharps in the key of A MAJOR. These are F , C , G .

A Major

This is the Key Signature of E FLAT MAJOR.

There are three flats in the key of E FLAT MAJOR. These are Bb, Eb, Ab.

E♭ Major

2. *WRITING*

Write the name of the key signature in the box under each of the following:

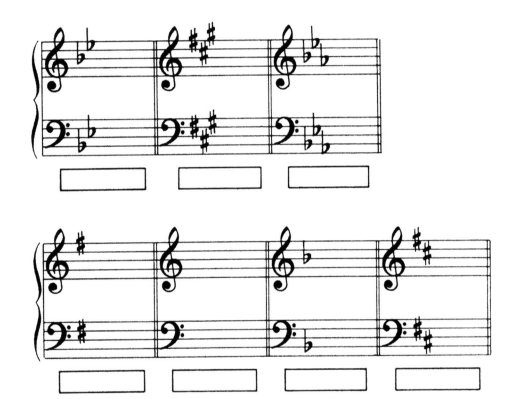

3. *COUNTING*

Put in the time signature and number the counting in each measure.

4. SPELLING

Print the words these notes spell
in the boxes under them.

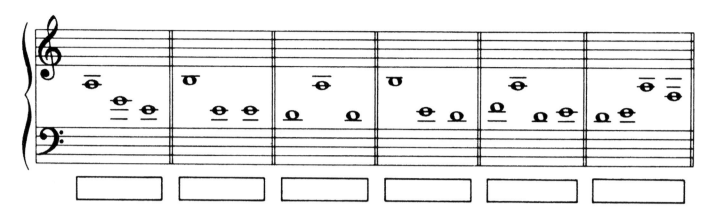

5. DRAWING

Draw a circle around all
sixteenth notes and six-
teenth rests.

6. GAME

JIG SAW PUZZLES

Draw an arrow from each Puzzle
Half in Column One to its matching half in Column Two.

Each Puzzle Half in Column One
has a rest inside it. In its matching half in Column Two fill in a
note with the same value.

COLUMN ONE **COLUMN TWO**

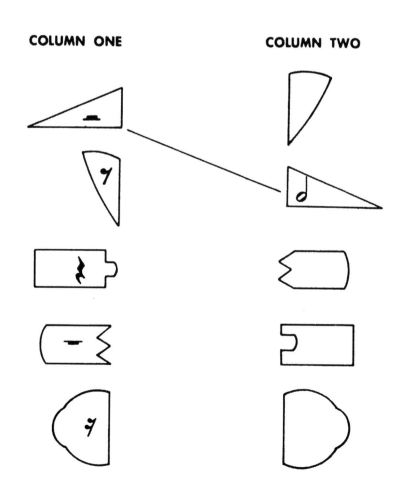

LESSON THREE

Pupil's Name _____ Date _____ Grade (or Star) _____

1. READING

HELPER

Study these LEGER LINE and SPACE notes.

A C E G B   B D F A C

These are above the staff.   These are below the staff.

E C A F D   D B G E C

As you read these Leger Line and Space notes, print their letter names in the boxes.

2. WRITING

Write the number of sharps or flats in each key signature and then name them in correct order.

F MAJOR has — 1 Flat ......Bb	B FLAT MAJOR has — ......
C MAJOR has —	E FLAT MAJOR has — ......
D MAJOR has —	A MAJOR has — ......
G MAJOR has —	

4. COUNTING

Join some notes together (in all but the last measure of each line) to give each measure the correct number of beats. Have some sixteenth notes in every measure you change.

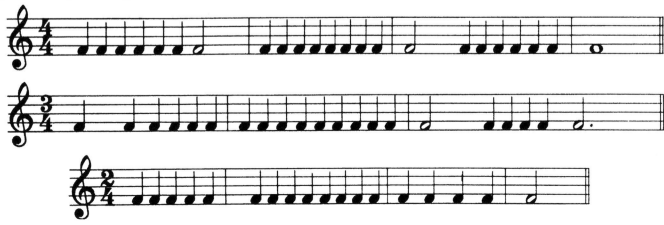

4. SPELLING

Spell correctly as you write the
meaning of the following words:

Tempo _____   Fine _____   Giocoso _____

Dolce _____   Allegro _____   Moderato _____

Andante _____   Marcato _____

5. DRAWING

Draw a whole line
of the following
Leger Line notes:

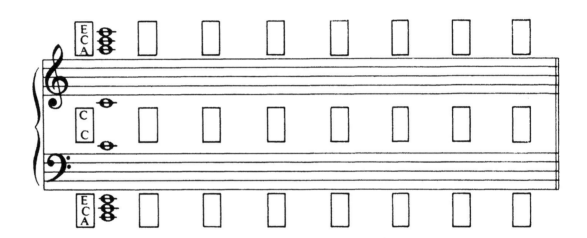

6. GAME

BLACK KEY PUZZLES

Draw an arrow from each
divided box with two letter
names to the matching black
key on the keyboard.

Fill in the two letter names
for the black keys in the
divided boxes.

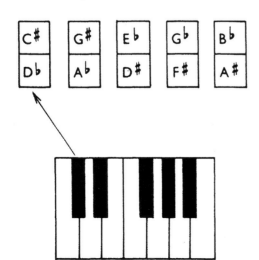

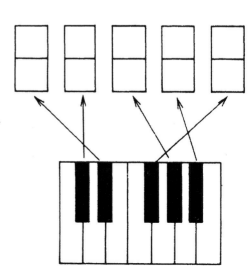

LESSON FOUR

Pupil's Name _____ Date _____ Grade (or Star) _____

1. READING

Read this Jingle aloud.
Watch the clef signs!

I LIK TO S   TH   IR S LY Y

ON   SUMM R   Y

TH Y LOOK SO R   UL IN TH SKY

S TH Y LY W Y

Fill in the missing letters to
see if you read the Jingle
correctly.

I LIK__ TO S___ TH__ __IR__S __LY __Y,
ON _ SUMM__R ___Y.
TH__Y LOOK SO __R_____UL IN TH__ SKY
__S TH__Y __LY __W__Y.

2. WRITING

Write these notes on
leger lines and spaces
above the treble staff.

A C E F G D B E G C

Write these notes on
leger lines and spaces
below the bass staff.

C E A G F D B E G C

3. SPELLING

Spell correctly as you write the
musical word for the following
meanings:

Gay and happy _____   The end _____

Softly and sweetly _____   March time _____

Slowly _____   Smooth _____

Time _____   Short, detached _____

4. COUNTING

Put the correct total of beats in each box.

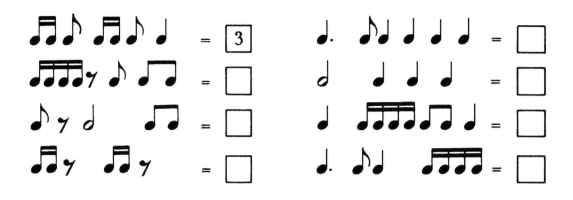

5. DRAWING

Draw an arrow from each word in Column One to its matching sign in Column Two.

COLUMN ONE

Gradually louder
Gradually softer
Tie
Slur
Hold
Staccato
Accent
Segno sign
Repeat
Triplets

COLUMN TWO

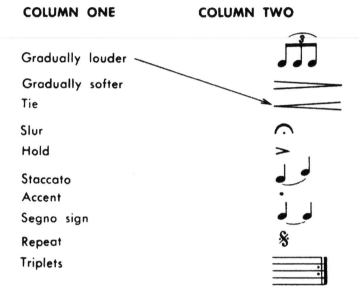

GAME
CATCH ME IF YOU CAN!

Make a check mark like this X after the correct answer for each of the following:

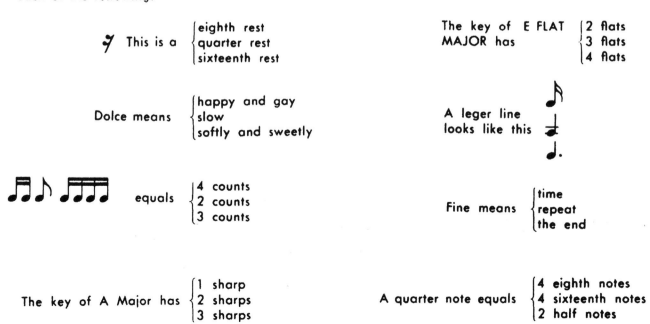

LESSON FIVE

Pupil's Name _____ Date _____ Grade (or Star) _____

1. READING

READ THIS ALOUD!

This is the Key Signature of E MAJOR.

There are four sharps in the key of E MAJOR. They are F#, C#, G#, D#.

E Major

This is the Key Signature of A FLAT MAJOR.

There are four flats in the key of A FLAT MAJOR. They are Bb, Eb, Ab, Db.

A♭ Major

2. WRITING

Write the names of the key signatures in the boxes below each one.

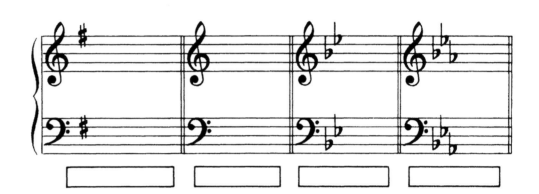

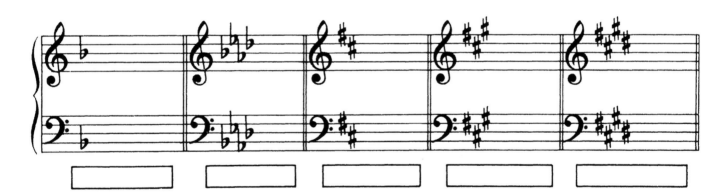

3. SPELLING

Spell the words the notes represent. Write them in the boxes above and below the staff.

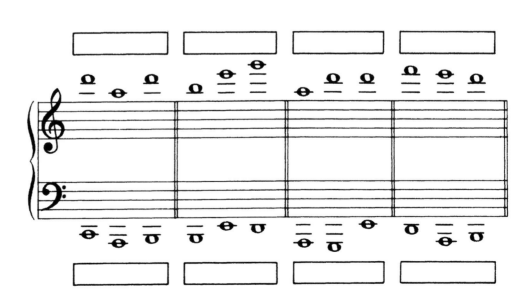

12

4. COUNTING

Put in the Time Signature and number the counting in each measure.

5. DRAWING

Draw an arrow from each group of notes in Column One to the correct Time Signature in Column Two.

COLUMN ONE   **COLUMN TWO**

$\frac{4}{4}$

$\frac{3}{4}$

$\frac{5}{4}$

$\frac{6}{4}$

$\frac{2}{4}$

6. GAME

TELEPHONE NUMBERS

Translate these notes into Telephone Numbers using the CODE.
Study the CODE and EXAMPLE.

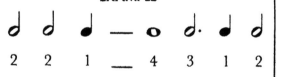

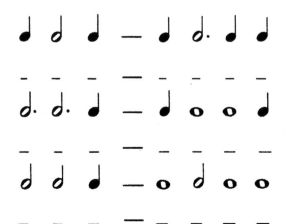

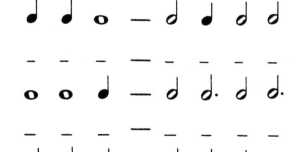

LESSON SIX

Pupil's Name _____ Date _____ Grade (or Star) _____

1. READING

READ THIS ALOUD!

Notice this Time Signature .... $\frac{6}{8}$

The top number tells how many beats in each measure — six.

The bottom number tells the KIND of note or rest that receives one bat — eighth note or rest.

In $\frac{6}{8}$ meter every note or rest receives twice as many beats

as it would in ...... $\frac{2}{4}$ $\frac{3}{4}$ $\frac{4}{4}$ $\frac{5}{4}$ $\frac{6}{4}$

in $\frac{4}{4}$
- ♪ = ½ beat
- ♩ = 1 beat
- ♩. = 1½ beats
- 𝅗𝅥 = 2 beats
- 𝅗𝅥. = 3 beats

in $\frac{6}{8}$
- ♪ = 1 beat
- ♩ = 2 beats
- ♩. = 3 beats
- 𝅗𝅥 = 4 beats
- 𝅗𝅥. = 6 beats

2. WRITING

In Column Two, write the number of sharps or flats in each key signature in Column One.

In Column Three, name the sharps and flats in the correct order.

COLUMN ONE	COLUMN TWO	COLUMN THREE
C MAJOR	_____	_____
D MAJOR	_____	_____
A MAJOR	_____	_____
B FLAT MAJOR	_____	_____
G MAJOR	_____	_____
E FLAT MAJOR	_____	_____
F MAJOR	_____	_____
E MAJOR	_____	_____
A FLAT MAJOR	_____	_____

3. COUNTING

Put in the bar lines and number the counting in each measure of the following:

4. SPELLING

Spell correctly as you complete the following sentences:

They will [⌢] the tickets for us until Thursday.

The dance music has a strong [>]

Will you [:||] the program for us next week?

I wrote Grace a thank you [♩]

I like to take a [𝄾] after dinner.

I want to [♩♩] the magazines together.

There is a good [≣] of workers at the office.

The kitten has [♯] claws

The plains are [♭] and wide.

We found a [♮] spring in the forest.

5. DRAWING

Draw a circle around every "A" ◯

Draw a square around every "C" ▢

Draw a triangle around every "E" △

Draw a heart around every "B" ♡

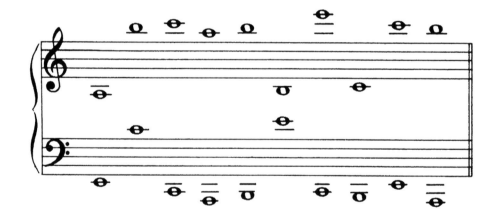

6. GAME

MYSTERY TUNE

This is the beginning of a well-known tune. Sing it to yourself (not playing the notes).

Write the name of the tune in the box above the music.

LESSON SEVEN

Pupil's Name _____ Date _____ Grade (or Star) _____

1. READING

Read this Jingle aloud!
Watch the clef signs!!

Fill in the missing letters
to see if you read the
Jingle correctly.

TH_ PIN_ TR___S _ROW SO V_RY T_LL, I S__ TH_M __R _N_ N__R.
TH_Y M_K_ M_ ___L SO V_RY SM_LL _SI _M ST_N_IN_ H_R_.

2. WRITING

Write each of the following
notes in FIVE different places.

Study the first one.

| A | C | E | B | F | D | G |

3. SPELLING

Spell the words that the
notes represent.
Print them in the boxes
above and below.

4. COUNTING

Put in the bar lines and number the counting for these three exercises. Watch the Time Signatures!

5. DRAWING

Draw these rests:

Draw 4 quarter rests =

Draw 4 eighth rests =

Draw 4 half rests =

Draw 4 sixteenth rests =

Draw 4 whole measure rests =

HELPER WORDS	
staccato	dolce
legato	fine
tempo	andante
sharp	flat

6. GAME

SCRAMBLED WORDS

There are mixed up letters in each box that may be made into musical words.

Print the musical word in the box after each group of "Scrambled Letters".

A C A
S T C
T O C
= STACCATO

M P
E
O T
=

L E
C O
D
=

T A
L F
=

N E
F I
=

P A
S R H
=

O T A
E G L
=

T E A
A N
D N N
=

LESSON EIGHT

Pupil's Name _____ Date _____ Grade (or Star) _____

1. READING

READ THIS ALOUD!

A HALF STEP is the distance between any key on the keyboard and the next nearest key up or down.

When the same letter name is used, the HALF STEP is called CHROMATIC.

This is a CHROMATIC
HALF STEP moving UP.

A to A#

This is a CHROMATIC
HALF STEP moving DOWN.

A to Ab

When different letter names are used, the HALF STEP is called DIATONIC.

This is a DIATONIC
HALF STEP moving UP.

A to Bb

This is a DIATONIC
HALF STEP moving DOWN.

Ab to G

Usually a helf step is from a white key to a black key, or from a black key to a white key. There are two places in the musical alphabet where a half step is from a white key to ANOTHER white key. These half steps are between E and F and B and C. (This is because there is no black key in between).

2. WRITING

In each of these boxes write "C" for Chromatic and "D" for Diatonic.

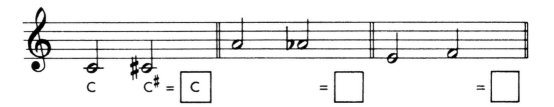

3. COUNTING

Make a check mark (X) for the correct time signature for each of the following:

4. SPELLING

Here are three titles.

In each box, spell correctly the musical term that will describe how you would play a piece with its particular title.

LULLABY

SOLDIERS' MARCH

THE HAPPY KITTEN

5. DRAWING

Draw a circle around every CHROMATIC HALF STEP.

6. GAME

FIND THE WHITE KEY TO WHITE KEY HALF STEPS.

Find the white key to white key half steps on this keyboard and make a mark like this (✓) to show where they are. The first one is done for you.

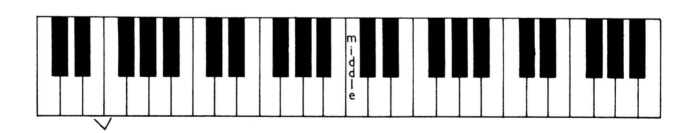

LESSON NINE

Pupil's Name _____ Date _____ Grade (or Star) _____

1. READING

READ THIS ALOUD!

A WHOLE STEP is a distance between two keys on the keyboard that is TWICE as far as a half step. It is the same distance as two half steps. In a whole step there is always one key in between the two outside keys. This key in between may be black or white.

Here are some whole steps. Print "W" for a whole step in the boxes below the notes.

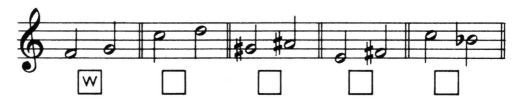

2. WRITING

Here are some whole steps and some half steps. In the boxes under each write "W" for whole steps and "H" for half steps.

3. COUNTING

In the measures in Column One, one note is missing.

In Column Two, put a check under the ONE note that would finish the measure correctly.

4. SPELLING

Spell the words these notes represent. Print them in the boxes above and below the notes.

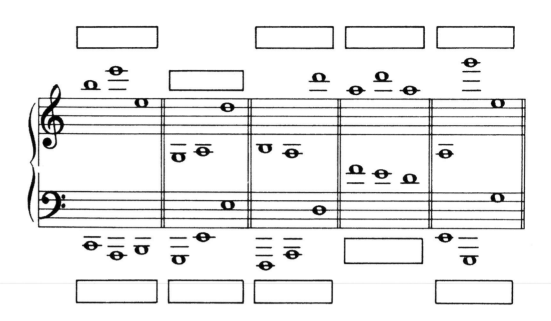

5. DRAWING

Draw a circle around every half step.

Draw a square around every whole step.

6. GAME

MYSTERY TUNE

This is the beginning of a well-known tune. Sing it to yourself (not playing the notes). Write the name of the tune in the box above the music.

LESSON TEN

Pupil's Name _____ Date _____ Grade (or Star) _____

1. READING

READ THIS ALOUD!

Here is the pattern for a Major Scale (using half steps and whole steps).

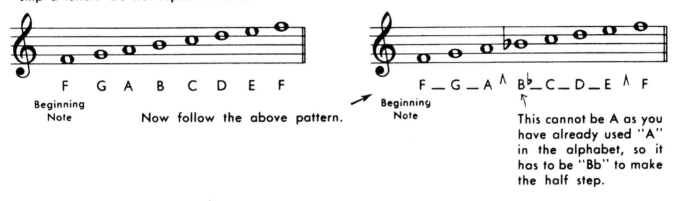

Begin on any note. Write a note on every line and space until you come to the same letter name on which you started. Name the music alphabet in correct order to one octave above. Do not skip a letter! Do not repeat a letter!

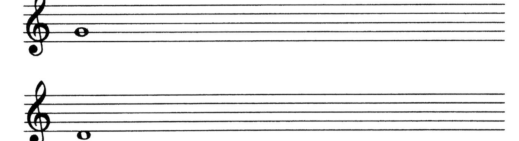

F G A B C D E F

Beginning Note

Now follow the above pattern.

Beginning Note

F _ G _ A ∧ B♭ _ C _ D _ E ∧ F

This cannot be A as you have already used "A" in the alphabet, so it has to be "B♭" to make the half step.

2. WRITING

Write a Major Scale beginning on the following notes. Mark the whole steps and the half steps.

3. COUNTING

HELPER: Dotted Eighth Note.

A dot placed after a note adds half of the notes' time value.

A dotted eighth note sounds the same as this — ♪♪ 1½ beats in ⁶⁄₈ You need to fill in missing part of the beat. What kind of note or rest in ⁶⁄₈ meter gets ½ beat? ♪ or 𝄾

Usually a dotted eighth note or rest is followed by a sixteenth note or rest to fill in the missing part of the beat.

Put in the bar lines and number the counting for the following:

4. SPELLING

Spell correctly as you fill in the words to compete the following:

The material is **_pp_** [|]

The band plays **_ff_** [|]

Her hair is long and legato [   ]

I like to take a [   ] before swimming.

Today I had a [   ] tire.

I do exercises on an acting [   ]

Will you please [   ] the question?

I will [   ] your seat for you until eight o'clock.

Please [   ] two yards of ribbon.

What tempo [   ] does your watch say?

5. DRAWING

Draw the pattern of a Major Scale.

6. GAME

FOLLOW THE LEADER

Copy these Key Signatures.

Print the name of the Key Signatures in the boxes below them.

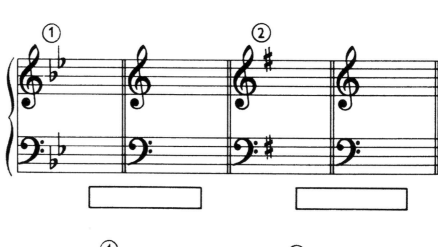

[   ]   [   ]

[   ]   [   ]   [   ]

LESSON ELEVEN

Pupil's Name _____ Date _____ Grade (or Star) _____

1. READING

Read this Jingle aloud!

Fill in the missing letters to see if you read the Jingle correctly:

MUSI_ IS _OR _V_RYON_,
N___R OR ___R _W_Y.
MUSI_ _RIN_S US H_PPIN_SS
_V__RY SIN_L_ __Y.

2. WRITING

Write the following Key Signatures:

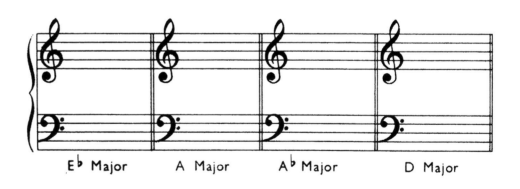

E♭ Major   A Major   A♭ Major   D Major

3. COUNTING

Each of the following represents one measure.

Put the correct time signature in the box before each one.

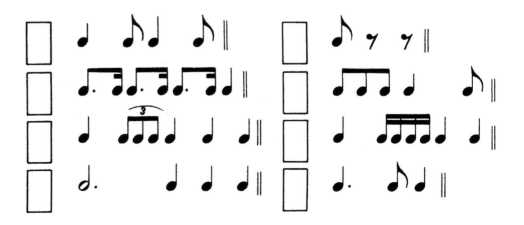

4. SPELLING

Spell the words that the notes represent.

Print them in the boxes above and below.

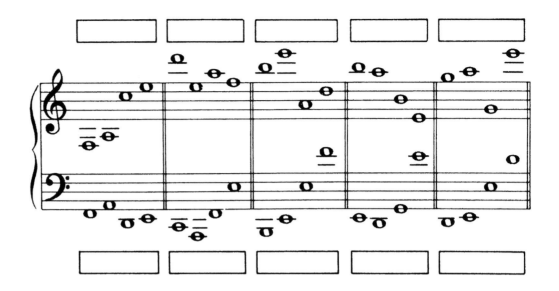

5. DRAWING

Draw a line like this ——— under every whole step.

Draw a mark like this ∧ under every half step.

6. GAME

CROSSWORD PUZZLE

Print the correct word in the PUZZLE that the CUE LIST calls for.

CUE LIST

Down

1. Abbreviation for gradually softer.
2. Time.
3. Abbreviation for gradually louder.
4. The end.

Across

1. Softly and sweetly.
5. Abbreviation for gradually slower.
6. Abbreviation for gradually faster.
7. Sign of silence.
8. March time and style.

PUZZLE

LESSON TWELVE

Pupil's Name _____ Date _____ Grade (or Star) _____

1. READING

As you read these notes, print their letter names in the boxes above and below them.

2. WRITING

Write the names of the key signatures in the boxes below them.

3. COUNTING

Number the counting under each of the following:

4. SPELLING

Spell correctly as you write
the musical word for each of
the following:

Softly, sweetly _____

Gay and happy _____

March time and style _____

Quick and lively _____

Slowly _____

Medium speed _____

The end _____

Time _____

5. DRAWING

Draw the following
musical signs:

Gradually louder _____   Gradually softer _____

Tie _____   Sixteenth note _____

Slur _____   Sixteenth rest _____

Triplet _____   Eighth rest _____

6. GAME

TWENTY QUESTIONS — TRUE OR FALSE

Print a "T" if it is true — or an "F" if it false
after each of the following:

1. Giocoso means slow. _____

2. A half step is the shortest distance we can move on the keyboard. _____

3. C to C# is a chromatic half step. _____

4. E to F is a whole step. _____

5. G to A♭ is a diatonic half step. _____

6. C# to D# is a whole step. _____

7. Dim. means gradually slower. _____

8. The key of A Major has three sharps. _____

9. This sign ➤ means gradually louder. _____

10. Dolce means softly and sweetly. _____

11. F# is the same as G♭ on the keyboard. _____

12. Four sixteenth notes equal one quarter note. _____

13. Marcato means march time. _____

14. This 𝄿 is a sixteenth rest. _____

16. In $\frac{6}{8}$ meter a quarter note gets one count. _____

15. In $\frac{5}{8}$ meter an eighth note gets one count. _____

17. This dotted quarter note ♩. gets 1 ½ beats in $\frac{4}{4}$ meter. _____

18. A dotted eighth note and a sixteenth note like this ♪. ♬ get one beat in $\frac{4}{4}$ meter. _____

19. This is the pattern of a Major Scale. _____   ○ — — ∧ — — — ∧
                                                      W   W H W W W H

20. Music brings us joy and happiness. _____

NOTES

NOTES